Copyright Page

ISBN 979-8-9893091-0-8 (hc)
ISBN 979-8-9893091-1-5 (sc)
ISBN 979-8-9893091-2-2 (cb)

Printed in the United States of America

Life Lessons

Advice for a Kid Like Me

By Gabriel Hamilton

Special Dedication

I dedicate this book to my nephews, D'landon and Dorian Taylor, and to any young man who wishes to become the best version of himself. I also want to send a special thank you to every man mentioned in this book and to anyone who has played an instrumental part in shaping me to become the man I am today. Because of you, I have grown in ways I would not have imagined and achieved things I didn't think were possible. I pray that the things you have taught me will continue to inspire a new generation of young men as they enter different phases in life.

Minister Cheatham, if you could teach only one lesson to a young kid like me, what would it be?

Have a relationship with God because through him, all blessings flow, and through him, all things are possible. Having a relationship with God is the very reason I am here today.

God helped me live through dangerous times in Vietnam. He had a plan for me, which kept me alive and allowed me to share his message every day.

Mr. Harris, if you could teach only one lesson to a young kid like me, what would it be?

Stand for something. Be a man of character. A man of principle. Standing for something starts with knowing what is fair and kind and is followed by the courage to do what is right, even when it may be difficult to do so.

This was my guiding principle while serving in the Marine Corps and in life. Being committed and having values, honesty, and integrity created a space for people to trust me and made it easier for me to take care of those around me. For me, it is the very foundation that a man stands on, and without a solid character, a boy never becomes a man.

Uncle William, if you could teach only one lesson to a young kid like me, what would it be?

Be disciplined. Being disciplined means having the self-control and determination to do what needs to be done, even when it's hard or you'd rather do something else.

You see, every day, I get up and work on what needs to be done. Sure, the work can be hard, I do get tired, and at times, I'd rather do something else. But the work doesn't get done without someone doing it. Discipline is what makes me do that work.

Dr. Polite , if you could teach only one lesson to a young kid like me, what would it be?

Get educated. Know that education is not about earning a certification or a degree. It is about learning what's important and applying that knowledge where and when necessary.

If it were not for scoring high on my ACT while in high school, my life might have been completely different. Scoring high allowed a poor child from Wichita to receive a full academic scholarship to Benedict College, which led me to attending and graduating from the prestigious Morehouse College.

That, in turn, led to many other opportunities, including becoming an educator and earning a doctoral degree. Education literally saved my life.

Mr. Downes, if you could teach only one lesson to a young kid like me, what would it be?

Know that timing is important. Understand that your timing doesn't depend on the world around you. Timing is not about rushing or waiting. It's about finding balance and knowing when to act.

It's like when you cross the street. If you walk out into the street when there is traffic, you might be hit by a car. If you wait for the signal or when there are no cars on the road, you can cross without danger. Life is very much like this. Knowing when to take action can make things much easier for you than forcing an action at the wrong time.

Mr. Johnson, if you could teach only one lesson to a young kid like me, what would it be?

Be a giver. Being a giver means to offer value in everything that you do. When adding value, remember to stay true to yourself and deliver more than expected . A man who does more than expected will always receive more than he gives.

Adding value has allowed me to build bridges and learn ways to achieve greater heights in life. For instance, I was able to create programs that benefit children in need, and that turned into a way of making a living for me and my family.

Chef Lew, if you could teach only one lesson to a young kid like me, what would it be?

Be flexible . The world around you is always changing, so you will need to change with it. Being flexible means having an open mind on how to achieve your goals and follow your dreams.

People use flexibility every day. Check out how you're able to bend and shape that dough. I learned this lesson in life. Early on, I followed the advice I was given and kept a routine. This kept me out of trouble, but it also limited me to what I could achieve.

As I grew older, I learned that I must be able to adapt to life and the things I encounter. As I started to adjust, my life became much easier, and success seemed to follow me everywhere I went.

Cousin Jerome, if you could teach only one lesson to a young kid like me, what would it be?

Know that failing doesn't make you a failure. Quitting is what makes you a failure. What makes you who you truly are is what you do consistently over time.

Like many men, I have failed. In fact, I have failed a lot. But that doesn't make me a failure. Every time I get knocked down, I learn. Then I get up and use what I've learned to get one step closer to achieving my goals. If I quit after I get knocked down, then I've failed, and that goal will never be reached. Also know that trouble is easy to get into, but hard to get out of.

Mr. Trey, if you could teach only one lesson to a young kid like me, what would it be?

Relationships matter. Relationships carry you further and can open doors that skills cannot. These interactions and connections can allow us to grow while affording us opportunities that we might not otherwise have.

For me, relationships have helped me find opportunities that have benefited me and my family. In fact, relationships are directly related to a person's ability to create a living and become wealthy. So, make sure you choose the right friends, and always strive to reach your full potential.

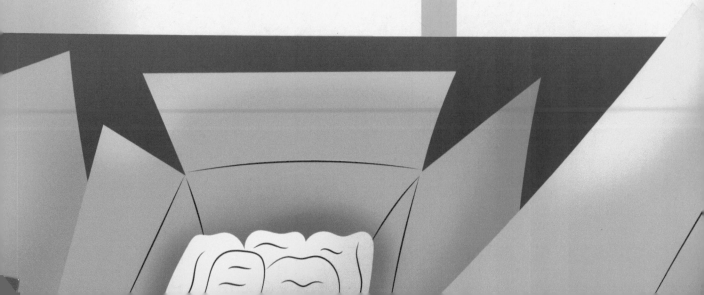

Mr. Hurst, if you could teach only one lesson to a young kid like me, what would it be?

Be loyal. Be loyal to the team that is dedicated to you, that invests in you, and that supports you. They are far more important than to those who praise or admire you.

For me, loyalty means building strong bonds between friends and family. Loyalty has always helped me to be a strong leader and to build strong bonds of trust. I mention this because it is easy in today's world to get caught up in the desire to be liked and lose focus on who and what is truly important in your life. So, stay focused on what is important, and be loyal to the team around you.

Mr. Smalls, if you could teach only one lesson to a young kid like me, what would it be?

Create opportunities. When you lack opportunity, take what you have at your disposal and create an opportunity. Also, when you have the power to create opportunities for others, create them.

A great example of creating opportunity could be setting up a lemonade stand to earn money. You could also use your lawnmower to cut grass. Once you've earned enough money cutting grass, you could purchase another lawnmower, creating an opportunity for a friend to earn money as well.

Mr. Sellers, if you could teach only one lesson to a young kid like me, what would it be?

Open your aperture. What I mean is to have broad vision and try to see things fully from other perspectives. Take time to read books, have conversations with people from all backgrounds, and seek out new experiences to truly embrace the beauty of the world around you.

Open-minded people are more likely to understand how others think and feel. Additionally, open-minded people have more fun because they get to experience the best parts of other people's cultures.

Dad, if you could teach only one lesson to a young kid like me, what would it be?

Start now and never give up. If it is important enough to you, you will figure it out. But if you never start, you will never achieve your dreams. So go, do, and be the man you desire to be.

About the Author

Gabriel was born in Manhattan, Kansas, in 1982. Very early in his life, Gabriel's mother, Janice, moved him and his two siblings to Wichita, Kansas, where they would remain through high school. Just before graduating high school, Gabriel signed up for the Army, and upon graduation, he answered the call to serve our nation. Since then, Gabriel has been a service member in the United States Army, traveled the world, and has earned numerous accolades and multiple degrees.

Most important to Gabriel is his family. Gabriel is the husband of Angiene Hamilton, the father of Nyah Hamilton, the son of Janice Jones, and the brother of Benjamin Jones III and Shantea Taylor. Gabriel's desire to write this book came from his experiences growing up and being mentored by amazing men. Throughout his life, Gabriel has learned that seeking advice from a wise council would not only make him better as a person, but it would unlock many mysteries of life. Therefore, he paid special attention to friends and mentors as they challenged him with ideas. Because of these actions, Gabriel grew into the well-rounded person he is known as today, and he uses that same information to challenge those who choose to listen.

Milton Keynes UK
Ingram Content Group UK Ltd.
UKHW051823110224
437540UK00003B/31